GET RID

AND AVOID BANKRUPTCY

by

Jim Arnold, Esq.

Attorney At Law

All Rights Reserved

Copyright © 2013 Jim Arnold. All rights are reserved, including the right to reproduce this book or portions thereof, in any form. You may not distribute this book in any way. No part of this text may be reproduced, transmitted, downloaded, decompiled, reverse engineered, or stored in or introduced into any information storage retrieval system, in any form or by any means, whether electronic or mechanical without the express written permission of the author. The scanning, uploading and distribution of this book via the Internet or via any other means without the permission of the author is illegal and punishable by law. Please purchase only authorized electronic editions, and do not participate in or encourage electronic piracy of copyrighted materials.

Legal Disclaimer

This book is intended to provide general information about the subject matter covered. It is not meant to provide legal opinions, offer advice, or serve as a substitute for advice by licensed, legal professionals. Although this book is designed to provide accurate and informative information in regard to the subject matter covered, the author does not warrant that the information is complete or accurate and does not assume and hereby disclaims any liability to any person for any loss or damage caused by errors, inaccuracies or omissions in this book. Laws and interpretations of those laws change frequently and vary state by state. It is understood that legal, tax, or other counsel should be consulted with regard to any questions presented in this book. If you want the help of a trained professional, consult an attorney licensed to practice in your state. The author shall not be liable for any special, consequential, or exemplary damages resulting, in whole or part, from the reader's use of, or reliance upon, this material.

About the Author

Jim Arnold is an attorney who graduated Cum Laude from Georgetown University with a degree in economics and received a Juris Doctor degree from the University of Virginia School Of Law. He is a member of the New York, Florida, Virginia and District of Columbia bars.

PREFACE

The reason I wrote this book is to help the many people who feel like they are about to go over a financial cliff and who see no way out of their overwhelming debt. It is written for those who have lost their jobs or who have had to take part-time jobs and for those who are disabled or have been through economic hardship because of medical problems, divorce, separation or death of a spouse and who are struggling to make ends meet. Whatever your circumstance or hardship, this book is designed to help you get the majority of your creditors and bill collectors off your back. It will teach you proven methods how to settle your debts by yourself and will give you specific telephone scripts along with letters and settlement agreements that you can use to substantially lower your debts for cents on the dollar.

When you are in debt, your phone may be constantly ringing with calls from credit card companies, collection agencies and other debt collectors and each day may find your mailbox filled with collection letters. Everywhere you turn you hear that you are not alone and that times are tough and that the economy will eventually turn around. Some even say that the "Consumers' financial condition continues to improve" (PR Newswire July 16, 2013). But, this news doesn't make you feel any better nor does it help you and your family to put food on the table.

Network and cable television, newspapers and magazines continually blare out the headlines to try to make people feel better. Yet, if one digs deeper, the true statistics can be found. The "official" unemployment rate announced by the federal government for June 2013 was 7.6%, for July 2013 it was 7.4%, and for August 2013 it was 7.3%.

These numbers, however, do not paint a true picture of unemployment in the United States. With respect to the "official" August 2013 unemployment rate of 7.3%, on September 6, 2013 the Washington Post reported that

> "Americans are participating in the workforce at the lowest level in 35 years, according to government data released Friday, as lackluster job growth fails to offset the droves of people who have given up looking for work. According to the Labor Department, the economy added a disappointing 169,000 jobs in August. In addition, the government lowered its estimate of the number of jobs created in June and July to 74,000 positions. The grinding pace of recovery has hollowed out the workforce. Government data showed that only 63.2 percent of working-age Americans have a job or are looking for one, the lowest proportion since 1978. Nearly 90 million people are now considered out of the labor force, up 1.7 million from August 2012."

Of the 169,000 jobs added in August, according to CNNMoney in a September 6, 2013 article, "many of the jobs came in traditionally low-paying sectors, with retailers adding 44,000 jobs and restaurants and bars adding about 21,000 jobs."

The New York Times reported on September 6, 2013, that "as of August, there were 7.9 million Americans who wanted to work full time but could find only part-time work. When these workers and people who want a job but have stopped looking are included, the total unemployment rate rises to 13.7 percent."

This 13.7% unemployment rate that the New York Times refers to includes men and women who are discouraged and have given up looking for a job or who have taken part-time work and is called the U-6 rate.

Since the recession began in 2008, it has been reported that 7.9 million jobs have been lost which is more than the 6.640 million jobs lost in the prior four recessions of 1980, 1981, 1990 and 2001 combined.

As reported in <u>The Washington Times</u> on August 5, 2013, "since January 2009 the country has added a net total of 270,000 full-time jobs, but it has added 1.9 million part-time jobs, according to the House Ways and Means Committee."

According to the Bureau of Labor Statistics, as of August 2013 there were 21 million unemployed and underemployed men and women. And, according to the Social Security Administration, as of July 2013, 41.194 million people over the age of 65 were receiving social security payments and 14,211 million disabled individuals under the age of 65 were receiving social security payments. This is in addition to the 7.222 million early retirees and young survivors receiving benefits. Thus, over 62 million individuals are receiving social security benefits.

"For people 10 years away from retirement the median savings is $12,000" and "of the people between 55 and 64, one third hasn't saved anything for retirement." <u>USA Today,</u> July 1, 2013.

The giant credit bureau TransUnion sates that the average credit card debt is $4,878 while the average balance on a credit card that carries a balance was $8,220. And those individuals seeking credit counseling had on average of seven credit cards and $24,000 of unsecured debt. <u>Fox Business,</u> July 30, 2013.

According to Bloomberg.com as reported on September 9, 2013, "forty-five percent of middle-class households earning between $50,000 and $150,000 per year spend all or more of their monthly earnings each month." Moreover, in a survey taken in October 2012 and as reported in CNNMoney, nearly one-third of the respondents or 30% said they planned to work until they are 80 or older.

And if these numbers and reports are not bad or depressing enough, a new study published August 29, 2013 in the journal Science, found that people preoccupied with money problems and who are in debt demonstrated an incredible drop in mental function equivalent to a 13 point loss in IQ.

In summary, this book is written for all those individuals who have lost their full time jobs, for those who have had to take part-time work because no other work is available, and for those who because of disability or other financial hardship such as medical bills, divorce, separation or death of a spouse or care of family members are drowning in a sea of debt.

Whatever the financial hardship that you may be facing, this book will assist you in substantially lowering you debt for cents on the dollar. It will specifically teach you how to settle your debts by yourself and will give you the telephone scripts, letters and settlement agreements to do so.

This book is not for those who have a job and can afford to pay their bills but just want to not pay their creditors so they can buy a new car or boat. This book is also not for those consumers who are thinking of using debt settlement or debt negotiation or debt relief companies. As set forth in the reasons given in Chapter 3, it will be explained why it is not advisable nor recommended to use these debt settlement companies.

The author is an attorney who for over 25 years has helped financially distressed individuals and small businesses settle debts for cents on the dollar and he has also trained individuals to do it themselves.

INTRODUCTION

Although this book is written to assist you with reducing your debts without the need of going into bankruptcy, a few words about bankruptcy are probably appropriate at this time. Bankruptcy is a procedure under federal law by which individuals who owe more than they can pay back can either have their debs canceled or work out a payment plan.

According to <u>Forbes</u> in a March 25, 2010 article entitled "Top Five Reasons Why People Go Bankrupt," the number one reason is medical expense, which represents 62% of all personal bankruptcies. Reason number two is job loss and reason number 3 is poor or excess use of credit. Reason number four is because of divorce or separation and reason number five includes unexpected expenses such as loss of property due to theft or casualty, such as earthquakes, floods or tornadoes where the owner has no insurance.

In the twelve months ending March 31, 2013, bankruptcy cases totaled 1,170,324.

There are three types of bankruptcies available to individuals, Chapter 7, Chapter 11, and Chapter 13.

Chapter 7 is also known as a straight bankruptcy or liquidation and it eliminates all of your debts. It allows the individual to retain certain exempt properties, with all remaining properties being sold or liquidated. The cost of a Chapter 7 bankruptcy varies from state to state but typically costs between $800 and $2500. For the 12 months ending March 31, 2013, there were 804,885 Chapter 7 bankruptcies.

A Chapter 11 bankruptcy allows you to restructure payment of your debts. Generally the costs for a Chapter 11 bankruptcy are prohibitive for an individual and can run from a conservative estimate of $10,000 to over $100,000. It is primarily used by organizations and businesses.

A Chapter 13 bankruptcy allows a debtor with a regular source of income to pay off his or her debts, often over 3 to 5 years. The cost of a Chapter 13 bankruptcy varies from state to state but typically costs between $2000 and $3500. For the twelve months ending March 31, 2013, there were 355,081 Chapter 13 bankruptcies.

Many attorneys offer a free consultation if you are considering bankruptcy. In light of the complexity of the 2005 Bankruptcy Abuse Prevention and Consumer Protection Act, and the most basic bankruptcy summary as set forth above, it is strongly urged that you seek out a local bankruptcy attorney if you are considering a bankruptcy. And remember that bankruptcy does not relieve an individual of all debts and that some debts still must be paid such as taxes, spousal and child support, and student loans, among others.

Considering the cost of a bankruptcy, CNNMoney on May 7, 2012 wrote an article entitled "Too Broke to go Bankrupt." The article went on to say that between 200,000 and one million consumers did not have bankruptcy as an option due to the steep costs. The article also stated that bankruptcy was not something that an individual should try to do alone without a bankruptcy lawyer because "it is too complicated now" and "make a mistake and your case is dismissed."

If you are interested in contacting a bankruptcy attorney, check out the National Association of Consumer Bankruptcy Attorneys which site will enable you search online for a bankruptcy attorney by city, state and zip code.

There is also an excellent May 21, 2013 article in FoxBusiness entitled "How to Pick a Bankruptcy Attorney." The article suggests that you meet with a few different attorneys to discuss your personal situation and to look for three main qualities during the consultation with each attorney that you interview. 1. "They discuss alternate resolutions" (Chapter 7 and Chapter 13). 2. "They display a passion for the process"). 3. "They hear and understand you" (that they "exhibit a desire to understand your specific situation and goals"). The article goes on to recommend that you "avoid ultra-low-rate bankruptcy mills that advertise heavily and crank out the cases. They usually only have a few lawyers and a large number of legal assistants."

There is an alternative to bankruptcy to reduce your debts, however, and that is what this book is about. That process is called debt settlement or debt negotiation. The purpose of the remainder of this book is to explain and teach you the principles of debt settlement and debt negotiation and to teach you how to use debt settlement to substantially lower your debts by yourself. The techniques that you are about to learn work whether you have personal debts or business debts.

At this point you may be asking why a creditor would want to take a lesser amount than what is owed. Creditors understand that they are likely to get no or very little money if the debtor goes into bankruptcy. If an account is more than six months old, the likelihood increases that the creditor or business will not be able to collect the debt from the debtor. Hence, many creditors are willing to take a lesser amount from the debtor.

TABLE OF CONTENTS

Chapter 1: WHAT ARE DEBTS?

Chapter 2: WHAT DEBTS ARE WORTH SETTLING?

Chapter 3: WHY YOU DO NOT WANT TO USE A DEBT SETTLEMENT OR DEBT NEGOTIATION OR DEBT RELIEF COMPANY TO SETTLE YOUR DEBTS?

Chapter 4: WHAT IS THE BEST WAY TO GET RID OF MY DEBT WHILE AVOIDING BANKRUPTCY?

Chapter 5: WHAT SHOULD I SAY ON THE TELEPHONE?

Chapter 6: WHAT OBJECTIONS WILL I FACE AND HOW SHOULD I RESPOND?

Chapter 7: RELEASES AND MAKING PAYMENTS

Chapter 8: RESTRICTIVE ENDORSEMENT APPROACH ONLY

Chapter 9: CREDIT AFTER SETTLEMENT

Chapter 10: CONCLUSION

Chapter 11: FORMS, LETTERS AND AGREEMENTS

DEBT SETTLEMENT FORM

DEBT SUMMARY FORM

SAMPLE LETTER FOR SETTLEMENT IN FULL

RELEASE & SETTLEMENT AGREEMENT FOR SETTLEMENT IN FULL

SAMPLE LETTER FOR MONTHLY PAYMENTS SETTLEMENT

RELEASE & SETTLEMENT AGREEMENT MAKING MONTHLY PAYMENTS

RELEASE & SETTLEMENT AGREEMENT WHEN THE MATTER IS IN COURT AND DEBTOR HAS BEEN SUED BY CREDITOR

RESTRICTIVE ENDORSEMENT FOR BACK OF PERSONAL CHECK WITHOUT HAVING A SETTLEMENT AGREEMENT

RESTRICTIVE ENDORSEMENT FOR BACK OF CASHIER'S CHECK OR MONEY ORDER WHEN SETTLEMENT PAYMENT IS TO BE MADE TO CREDITOR

Chapter 1

WHAT ARE DEBTS?

"D-E-B-T. It's one of the most dreaded four-letter words in the country these days- and dealing with it often leaves you wishing you could just snap your wallet shut, tell the company 'too bad, I'm not forking over my hard-earned cash to you' and move on." <u>Forbes</u>, "3 Debts to Consider Not Paying Off," June 6, 2012.

Napoleon Hill (1883-1970), the American author and widely considered to be one of the greatest writers of all time on achievement and success, is quoted as saying that

> "No man can do his best work, no man can express himself in terms that command respect, no man can either create or carry out a definite purpose in life, with heavy debt hanging over his head."…"Most men who develop the habit of debt will not be so fortunate as to come to their senses in time to save themselves, because debt is something like quicksand in that it has a tendency to draw its victim deeper and deeper into the mire…. The man who becomes hopelessly in debt is seized with this poverty fear, his ambition and self-confidence becomes paralyzed, and he sinks gradually into oblivion."

Simply stated, a debt is an obligation to pay a business or individual money that is owed. Some debts can be quite large like the debt on your home or car or to a hospital, while others may be very small like a magazine subscription that you have subscribed to but have not yet paid, or a month's dues to a health club that you have not paid.

There are generally two types of debt, secured debt and unsecured debt. When you have given an interest in the property or item to the business or creditor you have a "secured debt." The property that you have given an interest in is called the "collateral" and it adds "security" to the creditor that you will pay the debt. If you do not pay the secured debt, the lender or creditor can come and take the property or collateral back from you. The two best examples of secured loans are your house and your car. If you do not pay on your car loan, your car is repossessed. And, if you do not make your house payment, your house is foreclosed on and the lender takes your house back.

Unsecured debts are those where the lender does not have collateral. There is nothing to take back if you do not pay. Unsecured debts include credit card charges and most other debts that you are familiar with. If you continue not to pay, the creditor has basically only one option to get the money from you. That is, to sue you, get a judgment for the money that you owe and try to collect on that judgment.

The Forbes article dated June 6, 2012 and referenced above, suggests that "you'll want to first pay for the essentials (like food and housing) that most impact your life, as well as your car (if you need it to get to or find work), and the things you can go to jail for not paying (like alimony and taxes) before your other bills," quoting Thomas Fox, Director of Cambridge Credit Counseling. Forbes goes on to state that "if you can't pay all of your debts, consider not paying off on of your so-called 'unsecured debts,' which are debts like a hospital or credit-card bill that aren't backed by an asset," quoting Andrew Schrage, founder of MoneyCrashers.com. "The reason: When you don't pay a 'secured debt' (like a car loan), which is backed by an asset (your car), you can lose the asset since the bank can repossess it, but in the case of your 'unsecured debt," there is no asset to lose."

Since the vast majority of the debts that you are likely to have are in the unsecured category, this book will cover techniques that have been effective in substantially reducing these unsecured debts. If you have a problem with a secured asset such as your house, it is strongly recommended that you contact a local attorney who specializes in real estate transactions, property foreclosures or consumer protection.

It was already mentioned in the Introduction that a good way to find a Bankruptcy lawyer is to go to the National Association of Consumer Bankruptcy Attorneys web site to search for a bankruptcy attorney. You can also find a lawyer who specializes in debt collection law through the National Association of Consumer Advocates. Another good source to locate an attorney is to use Martindale.com. To use this source, type in your city and debtor-creditor, foreclosure, real estate or consumer protection for the area of law. Martindale.com is the source that most attorneys use to locate an attorney in different parts of the country. It also gives client review ratings. You can also use FindLaw.com or contact your local bar association to locate a lawyer to help you with your secured asset debts and home foreclosure.

At this point in the discussion and since foreclosure has been mentioned, you should be aware that a significant change was made on August 15, 2013 by the U.S. Department of Housing and Urban Development with regard to all FHA approved mortgages in a document entitled "Back to work-Extenuating Circumstances." The document states that

"FHA is continuing its commitment to fully evaluate borrowers who have experienced periods of financial difficulty due to extenuating circumstances.

As a result of the recent recession many borrowers who experienced unemployment or other severe reductions in income, were unable to make their monthly mortgage payments, and ultimately lost their homes to a pre-foreclosure sale, deed-in-lieu, or foreclosure. Some borrowers were forced to declare bankruptcy to discharge or restructure their debts. Because of these recent recession-related periods of financial difficulty, borrowers' credit has been negatively affected. FHA recognizes the hardships faced by these borrowers, and realizes that their credit histories may not fully reflect their true ability or propensity to repay a mortgage.

To that end, FHA is allowing for the consideration of borrowers who have experienced an *Economic Event* and can document that:
☐ certain credit impairments were the result of a Loss of Employment or a significant loss of Household Income beyond the borrower's control;
☐ the borrower has demonstrated full recovery from the event; and,
☐ the borrower has completed housing counseling."

This new policy is effective from August 15, 2013 through September 30, 2016. Normally, individuals who had a foreclosure had to wait three years before they could qualify for a FHA loan, which require only a 3 ½% down payment. This new change allows borrowers who meet the above criteria to qualify for an FHA loan only 12 months after losing a house to foreclosure.

Chapter 2

WHAT DEBTS ARE WORTH SETTLING?

As stated in Chapter 1, the techniques that have proven most effective in settling and substantially reducing your debts work best with unsecured debts, which are the debts that most people incur. The following is a list of typical unsecured debts (this list is only a sample and there are other unsecured debts) that can be reduced by using the techniques that you will learn in Chapter 4 and the remaining chapters. These common unsecured debts are listed in alphabetical order, and are not in order of importance nor is the list exhaustive of all unsecured debts:

- accountant bills
- advertising agency bills
- ambulance service bills
- architect bills
- auto repair bills
- bank overdraft fees to banks which you no longer have an account with
- car service or limo bills
- cell phone bills
- chiropractor bills
- country club dues
- contractors' bills
- credit card purchases and advances
- debts that resulted from an auto accident claim
- dentist bills
- department store charges
- doctor bills
- electrician bills
- educational loans
- electric company bills
- employment agency fees
- funeral parlor charges

- furniture store charges (unless the store has a security interest in the furniture)
- gas station charges
- grocery store accounts
- health club dues
- hospital and clinic bills
- kennel charges
- insurance company bills
- landlord rent (except in states that allow landlord liens)
- landscape bills
- lawyers bills
- loans-unsecured from banks, finance companies and individuals
- moving company bills
- ophthalmologist bills
- personal loans
- pharmacy bills
- photography studio bills
- plumbers bills
- printing bills
- psychologists and psychiatrist bills
- restaurant accounts
- student loans (private student loans funded by banks or other private lenders)
- union dues
- unsecured personal loans/signature loans
- unsecured credit lines
- urgent care clinics
- utility bills
- veterinarian bills
- water company bills

It should be noted that some of the typical unsecured debts listed above can become almost like secured debts. For example, if a moving company still has your furniture and is not willing to give it to you unless you pay them, it is more difficult to settle the amount of money you owe them.

Although it is harder to negotiate with them, the techniques that you will learn in this book can still be tried.

Similarly, a golf club may lock up your favorite golf clubs if they have possession of them when you start the method given to you in this book. You should also note that some department stores may also make customers sign security agreements for expensive items such as furniture and appliances. Once again, although it may be possible to reduce and settle secured debts with the techniques that you are about to learn, for the most part it is more difficult to settle secured debts because the lender has the ability to take back or keep the property that you have given as collateral.

Chapter 3

WHY YOU DO NOT WANT TO USE A DEBT SETTLEMENT OR DEBT NEGOTIATION OR DEBT RELIEF COMPANY TO SETTLE YOUR DEBTS?

During these tough financial times, you may have heard on the radio or TV or received in the mail an advertisement from a debt settlement company on how they can reduce the amount you pay to your creditors by up to 80%. These may also go by the name debt negotiation or debt relief companies. These debt settlement companies advertise that they can substantially reduce your debt.

Debt settlement companies are different than debt consolidation companies. Debt consolidation companies are primarily owned by the credit card companies and act as a third-party for you in that you make a monthly payment to them and then they pay your bills for you. You still have to pay off the entire balance, so there is neither relief nor reduction of the debt when you use a debt consolidation company.

As for debt settlement companies, they may advertise "reduce your debt up to 65% or 80%" or "get out of debt in in less than six months." They promise to reduce your debts by making a lump sum settlement offer and in turn you pay them a fee. They claim their fee is only a percentage of the money that they will "save" you. They oftentimes collect their fee up front and many times your creditors will not see any of it. **As you will see in the remaining chapters of this book, you can do this debt settlement yourself for free without the need of paying a debt settlement or debt negotiation company.**

Dave Ramsey is a financial author, personal money management expert and is an extremely popular national radio personality, television host and motivational speaker who has many good ideas on his website about reducing your debts. As Dave Ramsey has said,

> "One of the top areas of financial things that are complained about to the Federal Trade Commission as being a scam is debt settlement companies. They are hugely unethical. There are legit ones, but as a group, they are bad. All their fees come up front. You'll pay them thousands in fees before they do anything. They've told you not to pay your bills and that totally destroys your credit…The problem has been that they collect their fees up front, and then go along like that, and they won't return your calls. They don't put forth the effort that you will in settling your debt." Dave Ramsey and many other financial experts recommend that you reduce your debt by you directly negotiating with your creditors.

A bankruptcy attorney who practices in New York and New Jersey, Daniel Gershburg, Esq., has said that

> "at the end of the day, in my opinion, you are FAR FAR worse off ever paying these people [debt settlement companies] a penny of your money than doing this on your own or filing for Bankruptcy for literally a fraction of the cost." And, in writing about one of the major companies engaged in debt settlement that was shut down by the Federal Trade Commission, Mr. Gershburg stated that "the company's court records show that only 1.4% of the consumers who signed up for the program ever completed it. 1.4%!!!"

Suze Orman, financial author, financial advisor, motivational speaker and television host, in her Ultimate Money Lessons asks,

> "Is Debt Consolidation Right For You? If you are hopelessly behind in your credit card payments and you see no way out, it can be tempting to sign up with a debt consolidation firm that promises to make everything better. But you need to stand in the truth: signing up with a debt consolidation firm will likely make your financial life even worse." In another article entitled "Managing Debt," Suze Orman suggest that "you should call a lawyer and find out what she can do to help you settle the outstanding balance."

On the New York Attorney General's web site, it states that

> "many debt settlement companies make promises that they simply cannot keep and leave consumers in worse financial state then when they began…most consumers who sign-up with the debt settlement companies find the companies' promises are empty…Be wary of debt settlement companies that promise to obtain settlements for much less money than consumers owe. Many debt settlement companies misrepresent their typical results and their success rates."

And, on the Illinois Attorney General web site, Attorney General Lisa Madigan states that

> "Debt settlement companies advertise that they can settle all of your credit card debt in two to three years for only a fraction of what you owe. Do **not** fall for this come-on."

In an extensive report entitled "Profiteering From Financial Distress: An Examination Of The Debt Settlement Industry" by the Civil Court Committee, Consumer Affairs Committee of the New York City Bar dated May 2012, the Committee reported that

> "Debt settlement companies have emerged as declining incomes and rising living costs have led consumers to see their debts increase...Many debt settlement service providers aimed their marketing efforts at financially distressed consumers with a minimum of $5,000 to $10,000 in debt, and began charging them advance fees shortly after they enrolled. Paying off the advanced fees could take many months, during which time these businesses advised consumers not to pay creditors, resulting in defaulted accounts, triggering spikes in interest rates and other penalties, mounting debt, damaged credit, and stepped up collection efforts, including the filing of collection lawsuits. Creditors often intensified debt collection efforts following consumers' enrollment in debt settlement programs and their ensuing default."

The Committee went on to describe suits brought against debt settlement companies by the Federal Trade Commission as well as the Banking Departments and Attorney Generals in the following states: Arizona, California, Colorado, Florida, Idaho, Illinois, Maine, Minnesota, New York, Tennessee, Texas, Vermont and West Virginia.

Even the Federal Government's Federal Trade Commission (FTC) has weighed in on settling credit card debt.

"If you've maxed out your credit cards and are getting deeper in debt, chances are you're feeling overwhelmed. How are you ever going to pay down the debt? Now imagine hearing about a company that promises to reduce – or even erase – your debt for pennies on the dollar. Sounds like the answer to your problems, right?

The Federal Trade Commission (FTC), the nation's consumer protection agency, says slow down, and consider how you can get out of the red without spending a whole lot of green."

The FTC goes on to say

"Beware of Debt Settlement Scams. Some companies offering debt settlement programs may engage in deception and fail to deliver on the promises they make — for example, promises or 'guarantees' to settle all your credit card debts for, say, 30 to 60 percent of the amount you owe. Other companies may try to collect their own fees from you before they have settled any of your debts — a practice prohibited under the FTC's Telemarketing Sales Rule (TSR) for companies engaged in telemarketing these services. Some fail to explain the risks associated with their programs: for example, that many (or most) consumers drop out without settling their debts, that consumers' credit reports may suffer, or that debt collectors may continue to call you." The FTC goes on to say "**negotiate directly with your**

credit card company, work with a credit counselor, or consider bankruptcy."

As the above experts advise, it is probably better not to use a debt settlement company to settle your debts. You will learn in the remaining chapters, that the best way to settle your debt is to do it yourself or with the help of a friend. The obvious question then becomes how do I do it?

Chapter 4

WHAT IS THE BEST WAY TO GET RID OF MY DEBTS WHILE AVOIDING BANKRUPTCY?

The procedures that you are about to learn have been used by distressed individuals and companies for many years with a great deal of success to settle many kinds of unsecured debt. Although the following procedures and techniques can be learned and undertaken by the individual that is having serious financial problems and is in debt, it sometimes has been found to work best where an independent individual or relative or friend makes the call on behalf of the debtor. If you desire, you can also hire a debtor-creditor attorney, consumer attorney or bankruptcy attorney to make the calls and settle the debt for you.

Typically the person who owes money is going through a great deal of anxiety and stress and oftentimes finds it just too emotional or difficult to explain his/her financial problems or conditions. It has also been found that some of the creditors themselves get very emotional, abusive or angry and sometimes resort to name calling.

In the spring of 2013 the author made a call on behalf of a debtor to a collection agency. Even though the author is an attorney, the collection agency individual called the author inappropriate names. (Note that the Federal Fair Debt Collection Practices Act prohibits debt collectors from using abusive, unfair, or deceptive practices to collect from you including harassment, the use of obscene or profane language or repeatedly using the phone to annoy an individual).

Thus, although the debtor can certainly make the settlement of his or her own debt by themselves (and many have done so), it may be best if one has "thick skin" and it is sometimes more effective when a friend, business associate, relative or other more independent person makes the call and settles the debt on behalf of the debtor. It is not impossible for you to act as your own negotiator in order to reduce your debt but you may be too emotionally involved to do so. And, it may be more believable to the creditor if another person attempts to explain why you haven't paid your bill and then attempts to negotiate a reduced amount for you. It should be noted that for some creditors, such as credit card companies, the company may ask for authorization from the debtor before they agree to speak to an outside person.

To get started and before you read the next chapter, you should get out all of your bills, invoices and collection letters that you have received and put them in a file alphabetized by creditor, store or business name. Then, on the Debt Summary Form included in Chapter 11 of this book write down your account number, telephone number of the creditor or collection agency, contact name of person if any, the date the money was due and total amount due. All of this information can be obtained from your last bill, statement or collection letter although you may have to call the creditor to have them email or send you the latest statement.

As a hypothetical example, your completed Debt Settlement Form could look as follows:

Creditor	Acct.	Phone	Contact	Due Date	$	Notes
Visa	123	212-###	Mr. Jones	5/1/13	$2000	
Jones Law	55	201-###	Mr. Smith	4/1/13	$3500	
Golf Club	321	857-###	Mr. Thomas	2/1/13	$1200	

                               Total $6,700

If you do not know the contact name at the creditor's business or collection agency leave it blank for now. It can be filled out when a contact person is located. Also, leave the notes section blank for now. As the creditor contact person tells you or your negotiator how much money they are willing to settle for, make notes to record the conversation.

After you have filled out the Debt Settlement Form, add up the total amount due your creditors. In the above example, it is $6,700. The total amount due could run from a few hundred dollars to hundreds of thousands of dollars. There is really no limit on the size of the debt that can be settled.

After you have determined the total dollar amount that you owe your creditors ($6,700 in the above example), the next step is to figure out the total amount of money that you have available to pay off your debts, while still allowing you and your family enough money to live on, eat and pay certain essentials such as your mortgage, rent or car payment. To go back to our example above, let's say that you calculate that you can come up with $1,700 to pay off your debts. Thus, you can pay off 25% of your debts ($1,700 amount you can raise) divided by ($6,700 amount of your debts) equals 25%. **Make sure that you have a calculator available for all of your debt negotiations.**

You may be asking where you can come up with the $1,700 to pay off your debts in the first place. One way is to check your cash, savings accounts and checking accounts or your equity line of credit on your house to see what you may have available. Another way is to borrow from relatives, friends or a finance company or bank. Or, you may have to sell that old car or boat or rare coins or that extra television or pool table that is not being used. Maybe you have a tax refund coming or you could have a garage sale. Another possibility is to speak to a pawnbroker or use Craigslist to sell various items that you no longer need or have use for.

The reason that I have been focusing on raising or finding cash or some money is because that the settlement techniques that you are about to learn require having some cash in the amount of 15% to 50% of your unsecured debts for the system to work. If you find that you have absolutely no money to work with and you cannot raise any money, these settlement techniques will not work and you are probably considered "judgment proof" which will be discussed later in this book.

To get back to our hypothetical example above, you have figured out that you have $1,700 to settle all of your unsecured debts. The next step is to take the file containing the bills, invoices and collection letters and the Debt Settlement Form and give them to the independent individual that you have chosen to reduce the debts for you—unless you have decided to make the calls yourself.

In the above example, if all of your unsecured creditors would take 25% on the dollar as payment in full, you would pay them all off with the $1,700 that you have come up with. Is 25% on the dollar reasonable to expect a creditor to take for the satisfaction of your debt? Experience has shown that the vast numbers of settlements are in the 20 cents to 50 cents on the dollar range. Sure, some creditors will take 15 cents on the dollar or less because they have learned from experience that if you were to go into bankruptcy they would more than likely as an unsecured creditor get 5 cents on the dollar or nothing and it could take them years to find out. Others may demand 90% or 100% of what you owe and these may eventually end up at 60% or 70%.

You should, however, stick to your amount (25% in our example), and not be too quick to settle with those that want higher amounts because experience has shown that most creditors usually end up settling for 20% to 50% of the debt owed. As will be seen later in this book, your negotiator or you can always go back later to those creditors who insist on receiving more that 50% on the dollar.

An extreme example of the lowest percentage that a creditor ever took in all the many years that the author has been doing this work involved a debt ten years ago of $154,000 that was incurred by a 75 year old man for plumbing work allegedly done on his farm house. The plumbing contractor had actually filed a mechanic's lien (a security interest on the title to the property) on the farm house but eventually accepted $3,500 as payment in full which amounted to a 98% discount off the claimed amount. The contractor also removed the mechanic's lien. Now this was a particularly nasty, brutal settlement that took place over many months and it involved some sophisticated legal tactics that I will not go into to but it does show that nothing is impossible.

What percentage or dollar amounts do you or your negotiator or friend start out offering? Experience has shown that one should start out with a dollar amount somewhat less than what you have figured you can afford to pay, knowing that it may end up higher during the negotiations. It should be noted at this point that although the author has been talking in percentages and cents on the dollar throughout this book, <u>it is extremely important that all offers made by you or your</u>

negotiator must be made in dollar amounts and not percentages.

In the example set forth above, where you figured that you can afford to pay 25 cents on the dollar or 25% to get rid of your debts, it would probably be best to start out with 13 ½% or 15 ½% or 17 ½% of the dollar amount that you owe to the creditor and offer that dollar amount to the creditor (for example 15 ½% of the Jones Firm $3500 debt above is $542.50 to be offered in full settlement of the debt). Why an odd number? Experience has shown that people react better to odd numbers.

In most cases there is give and take back and forth until you arrive at a final settlement dollar amount that is agreed to. For example, the Jones Firm will probably come back to you after you have offered to pay $542.50 and offer to settle with you for something like $2700 or 77%. To that you or your negotiator should come up somewhat higher and say $647.50 which is 18 ½% of the debt. They will probably then counter with another figure like $2000. This goes on until an agreement is reached at an amount that is acceptable to you. And, although some settlements may be 15% and some may be 40%-50%, they should average 25% because that is what you have available to pay for your total debt as given in the above example. For the Jones Firm this means you should aim for $875 which is 25% of $3500.

To help simplify matters, you or your negotiator may want to use the Debt Summary Form found in Chapter 11 to figure out how much money is left over after each debt settlement. Thus, if you pay the Jones Firm $875 you have $825 left to settle with the other two creditors where you started out having a total of $1,700 to settle all three debts. If the ABC Golf Club settles for 30% of the $1200 debt or a settlement of $360, you would be left with $465 to settle the VISA bill ($1700-$875-$360= $465).

Once again, the above is given primarily as an example of how you should go about settling the debts. You may have one debt, or fifty debts. It doesn't matter what the total number of debts is. And, the dollar amounts of the debts can be in the hundreds of dollars or hundreds of thousands of dollars. The procedures are still the same.

The next chapter will go into what specifically you need to say to the creditor or the collection agency on the telephone.

Chapter 5

WHAT SHOULD I SAY ON THE TELEPHONE?

Before we start, let's say that you have calculated the total amount of the debt that you owe, what money you think you can come up with to settle these debts, and you have come to the conclusion that you have absolutely no money and cannot afford to give your creditors anything. In that case you only have two choices. One is to avoid or ignore the collection calls and letters and hope for the best that they eventually go away. If you do not have any assets or things of value that can be attached by your creditors after they get a judgment against you, you are considered "judgment proof." Black's Law Dictionary defines "judgment proof" to describe a person "against whom a judgment of a court will have no effect as they will not be able to pay a debt or to meet the demands of judgment."

The worst that can happen is that some creditor may try to garnish or attach your wages if you are working. The best that can happen is that what you owe is too small for them to worry about and they eventually give up on you. (Some creditors have determined that it is not worth the time and expense and effort to sue you if the debt is $1,000 or less).

Sometimes a creditor has a difficult time even finding a lawyer to hire who is willing to sue you if the debt is too small. And, contrary to what some people may think, there is no debtor's prison that you can be put in. A debtor's prison was a prison for individuals who were unable to pay their debts. These prisons were used from ancient times and were a common way to deal with debtors until about the mid-1800s in the United

States and Europe. The United States actually eliminated debtor prisons by federal law in 1833.

Now you can go to prison for certain debts such as nonpayment of alimony and child support where contempt proceedings may be brought against you, and for writing a bad check which is a crime. In addition, hiding assets before filing for bankruptcy is a crime with penalties up to $25,000 and or five years in prison.

It should be noted that you could be criminally prosecuted if you write a bad check to pay your debt so this is not a settlement method that you should ever consider, especially not to buy yourself time. At the very least your bank will charge you fees. Currently bad check fees typically range from $20 to $50 depending on your bank and state. (Some states allow for additional fees based on the number of checks or the amount of the bad check.) At the worst, your bad check could be turned over to the district attorney for prosecution. Criminal penalties vary depending on the state the check was written in and can include fines and up to ten years in jail, depending on the amount of the check and the state that you wrote the bad check in. If convicted, felony charges will also show up on your background checks which can affect your ability to get a future job or obtain housing.

To emphasize again, do not even think of writing a bad check.

The second alternative if you have no money to settle your debts is to call a local bankruptcy lawyer to help you to file for bankruptcy. But remember, you will still need some money to pay the bankruptcy attorney as mentioned earlier in this book.

In either of those two cases you do not need this book to settle your debts. But assuming that you do have some money (and maybe not very much), but enough to try these debt settlement techniques out to settle your debts, the following will get you ready to make the necessary phone calls.

You should have in front of you, or give to the person who will be making the calls, your Debt Settlement Form, and the file with the notices and collection letters and bills along with your calculator. With this material in hand, you or the person acting on your behalf is ready to do the following:

1. Call the creditor and ask to speak to a supervisor in collections unless you already have a name of the person to speak to. And remember that if a credit card company is being called, and you are not making the call yourself, be personally available to get on the phone to give permission to the person calling on your behalf to speak to that credit card company.
2. The following script needs to be followed by you or your negotiator once the collection person is reached:

"Mr./Mrs./ Ms. _____ [debtor's name] has informed me that he/she owes you $_____ on account number _____.You may or may not be aware that Mr./Mrs./Ms. _____ has had serious financial problems because of" [give actual examples that are truthful such as--he lost his job in September of 2011 and has not been able to find work; she had a serious operation last Winter and has many medical bills to pay; she lost her husband of 40 years last Summer and cannot pay her bills; he was injured on the job last Fall and is no longer able to work and is permanently disabled; she is a single mother without a job and has a child with major medical problems; he is not working and has two sick parents who live with him; her house has gone into foreclosure, etc. The idea is to give some truthful reason or reasons as to why the full amount of the debt cannot be paid.] "In addition to these problems, Mr./Mrs. Ms. _____ has ____ [give number] of other creditors like yourself all looking for money. I have been authorized by Mr./Mrs./Ms. _____ to offer you $_____ to settle this claim." [Start with a 13 ½% to 15 ½% offer. Multiply by dollar amount owed. So if you owe $1000, offer $135 (13 ½% x $1000 = $135].

Or, if you are making the calls yourself, "I am calling you about my account number _____ that I owe you. I have had had serious financial problems because of" [give actual examples that are truthful such as--I lost my job in September of 2011 and I have not been able to find work; I had a serious operation last Winter and have many medical bills to pay; I lost my husband [wife] of 40 years last Summer and cannot pay my bills; I was injured on the job last Fall and am no longer able to work and am permanently disabled; I am a single mother without a job and I have a child with major medical problems; I am not working and I have two sick parents who live with me; my house has been foreclosed, etc. The idea is to give some truthful reason or reasons as to why the full amount of the debt cannot be paid.] "In addition to these problems, I have _____ number [give number] of other creditors like yourself all looking for money. I have figured out how much money that I have and I can offer you $_____ to settle my debt with you." [Start with a 13 ½% to 15 ½% offer. Multiply by dollar amount owed. So if you owe $1000, offer $135 (13 ½% x $1000 = $135].

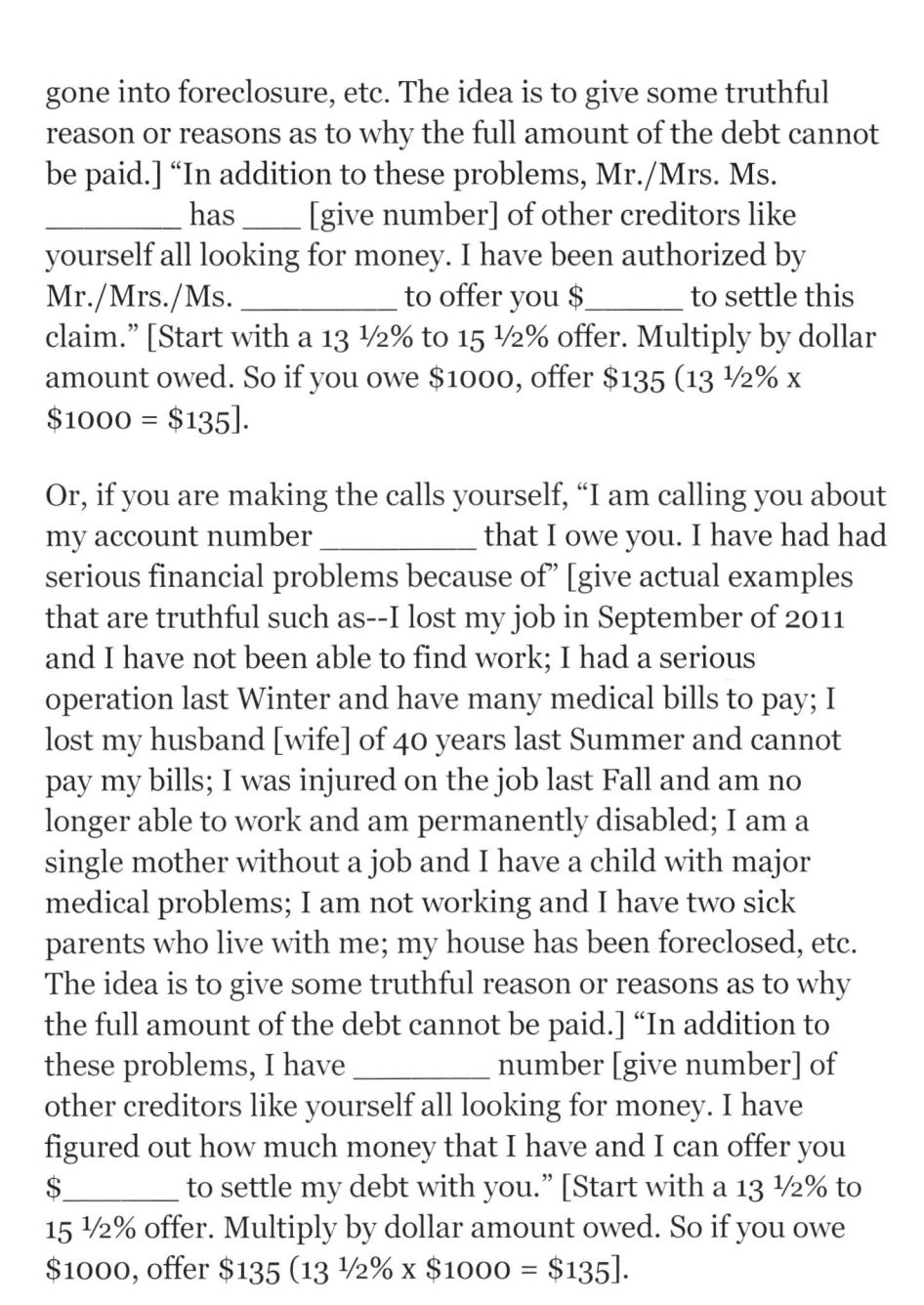

After this offer is made you or your negotiator should be quiet and let the creditor or collection person talk. The response back could be calm or not so calm by the creditor or collection agency. Sometimes the debtor is called names although a collection agency is not allowed by law to do this as mentioned earlier in this book. That is why it is recommended that another person make the call for you in order to be more objective. In any event remain calm no matter what is being said. The next Chapter will give you suggested responses based on what the creditor or collection agency says.

Chapter 6

WHAT OBJECTIONS WILL I FACE AND HOW SHOULD I RESPOND?

Based on experience, some of the comments or responses from the creditor or collection agency that will be made to you or your negotiator may be as follows, along with the suggested response that you or your negotiator can make back to the creditor.

1. Creditor Comment

A) "I will not take less than the full amount." Response by you or your negotiator—"I can appreciate what you are saying Mr. _____ [creditor's name] and can sympathize with your position, but the fact of the matter is that Mr. _____[debtor's name] [or, "I do not have"] does not have enough money to pay you. I am calling you first to make this offer to you, but if you are not interested I will go to the next creditor on the list and call you back in a month or so if there is any money left."

This response by you or your negotiator may cause the creditor to offer a reduced amount but more than what you or your negotiator wants to accept [the creditor may offer 50% or 70% for example]. To this you or your negotiator should say the following:

"As I already stated Mr. _____ [creditor's name], there is a very limited amount of money here. I wish I could give you 50% [or whatever the creditor offers] on the dollar but I just can't. Let me see though [pause], I may be able to get you $_____." [Give a slightly higher dollar amount than originally offered. You or your negotiator should get a feel for how the conversation is going. Do not give a percentage or cents on the dollar but always give a total dollar amount based on what you learned above. The whole idea here is to get a conversation going to negotiate a reduced amount].

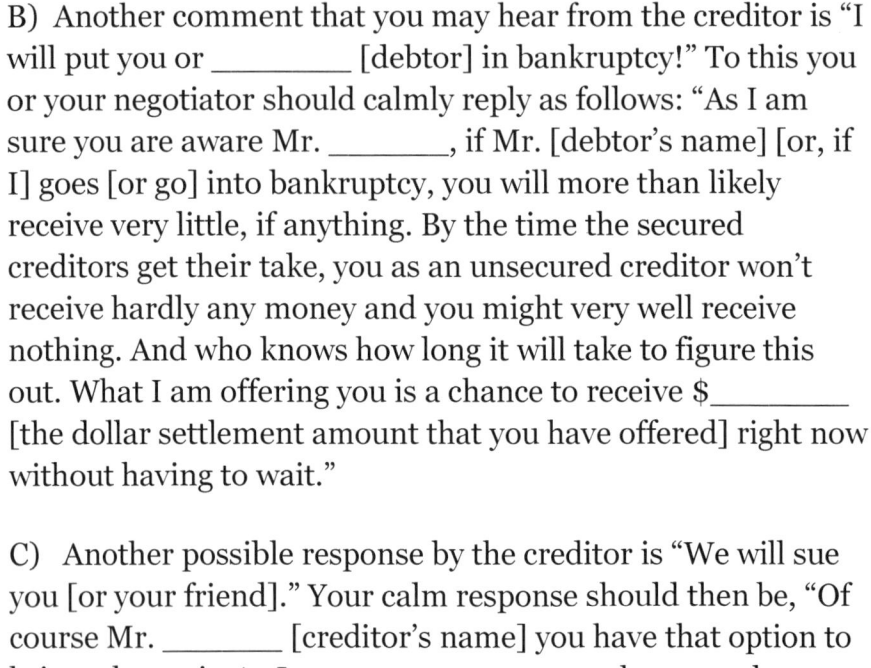

B) Another comment that you may hear from the creditor is "I will put you or _____ [debtor] in bankruptcy!" To this you or your negotiator should calmly reply as follows: "As I am sure you are aware Mr. _____, if Mr. [debtor's name] [or, if I] goes [or go] into bankruptcy, you will more than likely receive very little, if anything. By the time the secured creditors get their take, you as an unsecured creditor won't receive hardly any money and you might very well receive nothing. And who knows how long it will take to figure this out. What I am offering you is a chance to receive $_____ [the dollar settlement amount that you have offered] right now without having to wait."

C) Another possible response by the creditor is "We will sue you [or your friend]." Your calm response should then be, "Of course Mr. _____ [creditor's name] you have that option to bring a law suit. As I am sure you are aware, however, law suits take time and cost money. And if other creditors also bring law suits and do not take me up on this offer, I [he] will have no recourse but to see a bankruptcy lawyer and you are well aware of what happens during a bankruptcy. You as an unsecured creditor might get very little, if anything and it may take a long time. What I am offering you is immediate payment without having to wait."

The whole idea in the above responses is to have the creditor or collection agent engage in talking with you to negotiate a settlement to reduce your debt. You should in all instances figure out beforehand the absolute maximum that you can afford to pay. In some cases the creditor may have to get back to you or your negotiator and further discussions may take place. But in the end, the debt owed by you should be substantially reduced.

D) What happens if the creditor suggests a payment plan whereby you pay 100% of the debt over time? You or your negotiator should stick to your reduced amount and turn this down. The only time when you should consider a payment plan is if the creditor will not budge off 60% of the debt for example, and you can only really afford 30%. In that case, it may be worthwhile for you to enter into a payment plan if the amount being offered by the creditor is higher than you can pay, but you still desire to settle with this particular creditor.

E) And, once again, if the creditor is not willing to negotiate at all (this is rare), you or your negotiator should tell the creditor that you will call them back in a month or so after you have made offers to the other creditors and if there is any money left. In fact, you or your negotiator should then call that creditor, who refuses to negotiate, back in four weeks and say the following:

"Hi, Mr. [creditor's name], my name is _____ and I spoke to you 4 weeks ago concerning a debt owed to you by Mr. _____ [or by me] on account number _____. I tried to settle the debt with you at that time but you weren't interested. In the meantime, I have settled many debts for Mr. [debtor] [or I have settled many of my debts] with the other creditors and I am calling you back to see if you are interested in receiving a check immediately."

This should start up the settlement talks again and you or your negotiator should attempt to resell the creditor on why they should take less money now. If need be, this conversation can be done again in another four weeks. Sometimes the creditor gets tired of hearing all of this talk all the while not receiving any money and will eventually settle.

F) It should now be noted that the above procedures are primarily designed for situations where a law suit has not yet been brought against you, the debtor, and in cases where a judgment in a lawsuit has not been rendered by a court against you. In those instances where a lawsuit has been filed or a judgment has been rendered against you, you or your negotiator can still use the above techniques with the creditor or judgment holder or their attorney to reduce the debt owed. Just because a creditor brings a lawsuit against a debtor does not mean that the creditor will get any money from a debtor. Creditors know this very well and are usually agreeable to a settlement of a reduced amount even after a lawsuit has been brought. All that needs to be done is to modify the script as follows:

"Hi, my name is _____. I have been authorized by Mr. _____ [debtor] to contact you concerning an account that Mr. _____[debtor] has with you and which you have sued Mr. _____[debtor] for. The account number is _____ and the case number is _____. You may or may not be aware that Mr. _____[debtor] has had some serious financial problems because of [explain facts as set forth above]. Despite these problems, Mr. _____ [debtor] realizes that this money is owed to you and wants to make a payment. I have been authorized to offer you $_____to settle this claim. If we can reach an agreement, I would like you to dismiss the lawsuit [or

I would like you to vacate the judgment against Mr. _____ [debtor]."

Or, "Hi, my name is _____ and I am calling you concerning an account that I have with _____ [the creditor name], and the case number is _____. You may not be aware, that I have had some serious financial problems because of [explain facts as set forth above]. Despite these problems, I realize that this money is owed to your client and I would like to make a payment. I can afford to pay your client $_____ to settle this claim. If we can reach an agreement, I would like you to dismiss the lawsuit [or I would like you to vacate the judgment against me]."

The above conversation may take place with the creditor's attorney if known. This is assuming that you as debtor do not have an attorney representing you in the lawsuit. If you do, your attorney should attempt all settlement negotiations.

Finally, settlement negotiations may have to take place with a collection agency if the creditor has hired one to collect your debt. A collection agency is generally paid 15% to 33 1/3% of any amount collected from you. Collection agents will aggressively negotiate a debt because anything that they can collect they will be paid a percentage of. If they cannot collect any money from you and the matter goes to an attorney for suit, the collection agency usually does not make any money. Therefore, all of the procedures set forth above have been proven to have been successful with a collection agency.

Chapter 7

RELEASES AND MAKING PAYMENTS

Once the creditor or collection agent agrees with you or your negotiator to take a lesser amount of money than the debt that you owe, the next step is to send a letter and settlement agreement to the creditor which sample letter and agreement can be found in Chapter 11. And, after the creditor or collection agency returns the signed settlement agreement to you, you should immediately send a cashier's check or money order in the agreed upon amount to the creditor along with your signed copy of the settlement agreement. Make sure that you keep the settlement agreement signed by the creditor.

A second sample letter and settlement agreement can also be found in Chapter 11 which agreement should be used in those cases where a payment plan has been agreed to with the creditor.

In the event that the creditor has already instituted suit, a different settlement agreement dismissing the law suit can be found in Chapter 11, although in many cases the creditor's attorney will provide you with their own settlement agreement. And, once again, if you are using an attorney in any law suit that has been filed against you, it is important that you have your attorney handle the settlement agreement. It is also highly recommended that you hire an attorney any time that a creditor brings a law suit against you. A lawyer can help you formulate a defense and can guide you through the court proceedings. And remember that most lawyers offer free consultations. Chapter 1 discusses where to find an attorney to assist you.

Finally, after you receive the settlement agreement back from the creditor, the cashier's check or money order that is sent to the creditor should have the language set forth on the back of the check as can be found in the forms section in Chapter 11. This language should be put at the top of the check where it sometimes says "Endorse Here". Make sure that you make a copy of both sides of the cashier's check or money order before you send it to the creditor. If you do not put a restrictive endorsement on the back of the check, however, the signed settlement will protect you from further action on the debt. Always keep a copy of the settlement agreement signed by the creditor.

Chapter 8

RESTRICTIVE ENDORSEMENT APPROACH ONLY

In some cases it may be tempting for you to simply send a personal check for a lesser amount to the creditor with a restrictive endorsement such as "Paid in Full" on the back of the check or the restrictive endorsement similar to that found in the forms section of Chapter 11 without going through the settlement negotiations with the creditor as set forth elsewhere in this book. Although this technique may work in some states and the creditor will be precluded from coming after the debtor for the remainder of the debt, other states have said that it is unrealistic in the business world for a debtor to send what appears to be merely an installment payment, to have the rest of the debtor's debt eliminated simply because of a legend that the debtor puts on the back of a check.

This is a very complex area of the law and it is important to check your state as well as the creditor's state Uniform Commercial Code laws before attempting to send a check with just a restrictive endorsement on it.

Putting this restrictive endorsement on a check without a settlement with the creditor is very dangerous and it is not recommended. Whether or not a restrictive endorsement would be binding on the creditor or collection agency depends on numerous factors including your state laws, your contract with the creditor, and the creditor's actions once it receives your check.

Some states greatly restrict the use of restrictive endorsements while many contracts with businesses do not recognize restrictive endorsements and will treat the check as a regular payment. Some courts have ruled that the use of such an endorsement will only be valid where a settlement agreement exists between the parties or only if there is a good faith dispute between the parties. It is not a dispute if you never gave notice to the creditor that you dispute the bill but merely send a lesser amount with a restrictive endorsement.

Thus, if you are sending a check to the creditor to trick the creditor into accepting a smaller amount than you owe, you are playing a very dangerous game. It is much safer to negotiate and agree with the creditor as to the taking of a lesser amount and then send the suggested letter, settlement agreement and cashier's check or money order with restrictive endorsement as suggested in the previous chapter.

Before you just send a check with a restrictive endorsement on the back of the check without having agreed to a settlement with the creditor, it would be wise to consult with a lawyer to see what the law is in the state you are in.

Chapter 9

CREDIT AFTER SETTLEMENT

These days, so many people are trying to get their credit balances reduced with credit card companies that it is harder to settle than it used to be. Do not expect to reduce your balances just because you feel like it and it would make your life easier.

Debt settlement is specifically for hardships such as losing a job, medical emergencies, divorce etc. as set forth above. You must have a legitimate hardship reason for debt settlement to work. Don't expect to succeed if you are working but merely want to cut your debts in half so you can buy a new boat or motorcycle. In addition, settling your debt can lead to some negative situations such as lowering your credit score although chances are that it has already been lowered due to missed and late payments.

Credit card companies have the option of reporting your settlement to the credit agencies as "Paid in Full" or "Paid Settlement" or "Settled Debt" or "Settlement Offer." You always want to ask the creditor to report to the three major credit agencies that the debt has been "paid in full." Sometimes the creditor is willing to do this as a bargaining point even though you have not paid the full amount. You have leverage until the lender receives your check and you will see that the settlement agreements in Chapter 11 contain such language.

As for doing future business with the creditor, you may find that the creditor is willing to do business with you after a settlement on one condition—that you pay in advance with cash for the goods and services that you desire to purchase.

Don't expect creditors that you have settled with to extend credit to you although there are some businesses that may do so after a year or two of paying cash in advance.

There are a number of books on Amazon on the subject of repairing your credit. In addition, Suze Orman has a FICO kit and Dave Ramsey has a number of financial books including "The Total Money Makeover."

Chapter 10

CONCLUSION

In conclusion, it is hoped that the information that you have received in this book will help enable you to get out from under your debts. The techniques that have been given to you have been proven to work and can be used for individual debts incurred by you as well as for small businesses having financial difficulties. The main difference between the individual and small business settlements is that some creditors may ask for financial reports to see the true status of your financial condition if you are trying to settle a business debt.

I hope that this book assists you in reducing your debts and helps you in getting back on your financial feet.

Chapter 11

FORMS, LETTERS AND AGREEMENTS

DEBT SETTLEMENT FORM

Creditor	Acct. No.	Phone	Contact	Date Due
$ Due	Notes			

DEBT SUMMARY FORM

Creditor $ Settlement Amt.   Remaining for Settlement
Total $ Debts Remaining

Beginning with $_____
$_____

SAMPLE LETTER FOR SETTLEMENT IN FULL

Date

Your Name

Your Address

Your City, Your State, Zip Code

Re: Account Number or Reference Number _____

Dear _____ (or Sir/Madam if name is not known)

Pursuant to our telephone conversation where I explained to you my financial difficulties due to (repeat what you told him or her on the phone as to job loss, lay off, sickness, family problems, death etc.), I have been unable to pay the debt set forth above.

As we agreed on the phone, I can afford to pay you $_____ in full settlement of my debt and you have agreed to accept this amount. Please sign the enclosed settlement agreement and return it to me at the address listed above. As soon as I receive it, I will immediately pay the settlement amount in full by cashier's check or money order.

Thank you for your understanding and agreeing to work out this matter.

Sincerely,

(Your signature)

Your Name Printed

RELEASE & SETTLEMENT AGREEMENT FOR SETTLEMENT IN FULL

RELEASE & SETTLEMENT AGREEMENT

This RELEASE & SETTLEMENT AGREEMENT ("Agreement") made this ___ day of _____, 201(3) between _____[Debtor's Name] ("Debtor"), residing at _____, and _____["Creditor's Name"] ("Creditor") with an office at
_____
__.

WHEREAS, Debtor and Creditor have previously entered into certain commercial transactions under account number _____(the "Account"); and

WHEREAS, Creditor has alleged that Debtor owes Creditor $_____ under the Account; and

WHEREAS, certain circumstances have subsequently developed causing both Debtor and Creditor to desire to enter into this Agreement to settle in full the Account.

NOW, THEREFOR, based upon the mutual promises and covenants contained herein, the parties hereby agree as follows:

1. Debtor agrees to pay and Creditor agrees to accept $_____ as full payment for all amounts due Creditor by Debtor under the Account.

2. Debtor shall, at the time of receipt of an executed copy of this Agreement by Creditor, return a signed copy of this Agreement along with a cashier's check or money order made payable to Creditor within five (5) days of receiving the executed copy of this Agreement from Creditor.

3. The Creditor agrees to accept this cashier's check or money order from Debtor as payment in full.

4. Creditor agrees to report the Account of Debtor's as "Paid in Full" to all credit bureaus, and shall refrain from reporting any negative credit information regarding Debtor's Account.

5. This Release & Settlement Agreement sets forth the entire understanding between the parties, and cannot be changed, modified or canceled except by a writing signed by both parties.

6. If an agent signs this Agreement on behalf of the original creditor, the agent warrants and represents that the agent is the authorized signatory of the original creditor and has informed the original creditor of the terms of this Agreement and is authorized by the

original creditor to enter into this Agreement on its behalf, thereby binding the original creditor to all of this Agreement's terms and conditions.

IN WITNESS WHEREOF, the Debtor and Creditor have signed this Agreement as of the date set forth above.

DEBTOR

_____

CREDITOR

_____

Name and Title

SAMPLE LETTER FOR MONTHLY PAYMENTS SETTLEMENT

Date

Your Name

Your Address

Your City, Your State, Zip Code

Re: Account Number or Reference Number
_____

Dear _____ (or Sir/Madam if name is not known)

Pursuant to our telephone conversation where I explained to you my financial difficulties due to (repeat what you told him or her on the phone as to job loss, divorce, sickness, family problems, death etc.), I have been unable to pay the debt set forth above.

As we agreed on the phone, I can afford to pay you $_____ per month for a total of $_____ in full settlement of my debt and you have agreed to accept this amount. Please sign the enclosed settlement agreement and return it to me at the address listed above. As soon as I receive it, I will immediately pay you the first month's payment by cashier's check or money order.

Thank you for your understanding and agreeing to work out this matter.

Sincerely,

(Your signature)

Your Name Printed

RELEASE & SETTLEMENT AGREEMENT MAKING MONTHLY PAYMENTS

RELEASE & SETTLEMENT AGREEMENT

This RELEASE & SETTLEMENT AGREEMENT ("Agreement") made this ___ day of _____, 201(3) between _____ [Debtor] ("Debtor"), residing at _____, and _____[Creditor] ("Creditor") with an office at _____ _.

WHEREAS, Debtor and Creditor have previously entered into certain commercial transactions under account number _____(the "Account"); and

WHEREAS, Creditor has alleged that Debtor owes Creditor $_____ under the Account; and

WHEREAS, certain circumstances have subsequently developed causing both Debtor and Creditor to desire to enter into this Agreement to settle in full the Account.

NOW, THEREFOR, based upon the mutual promises and covenants contained herein, the parties hereby agree as follows:

1. Debtor agrees to pay and Creditor agrees to accept $_____ as full payment for all amounts due Creditor by Debtor under the Account.

2. Debtor shall be permitted to pay the amount in Section 1 by making monthly payments without interest in the amount of $_____ per month with each payment due on the first of each month.

3. Debtor shall, at the time of receipt of an executed copy of this Agreement by Creditor, return a signed copy of this Agreement along with a cashier's check or money order made payable to Creditor for the first month's payment within five (5) days of receiving the executed copy of this Agreement from Creditor.

4. The Creditor agrees to accept these payments in full satisfaction of all amounts claimed from Debtor.

5. If Debtor fails to make any one or more of these payments when due, then Creditor may proceed against Debtor either under this Agreement or under the Creditor's original claim against Debtor, or both.

6. Upon receipt by Creditor of the last payment as agreed upon in this Agreement, Creditor agrees to report the Account of Debtor as "Paid in Full" to all credit bureaus, and shall refrain from reporting any negative credit information regarding Debtor's Account.

7. This Release & Settlement Agreement sets forth the entire understanding between the parties, and cannot

be changed, modified or canceled except by a writing signed by both parties.

8. If an agent signs this Agreement on behalf of the original creditor, the agent warrants and represents that the agent is the authorized signatory of the original creditor and has informed the original creditor of the terms of this Agreement and is authorized by the original creditor to enter into this Agreement on its behalf, thereby binding the original creditor to all of this Agreement's terms and conditions.

IN WITNESS WHEREOF, the Debtor and Creditor have signed this Agreement as of the date set forth above.

DEBTOR

_____

CREDITOR

_____

Name and Title

RELEASE & SETTLEMENT AGREEMENT WHEN THE MATTER IS IN COURT AND DEBTOR HAS BEEN SUED BY CREDITOR

NOTE: When the matter is in court and the Creditor has sued you, the Debtor, it is sometimes more difficult to settle the case. It is strongly recommended that you seek a local attorney to assist you with the settlement agreement and/or defense of the law suit. With that being said, the following is a sample release and settlement agreement when the matter is in court. Specific courts that handle debtor-creditor matters can vary from state to state.

RELEASE & SETTLEMENT AGREEMENT

This Release and Settlement Agreement ("Agreement") is entered into between the following parties ("the Parties"): _____ [Plaintiff's Name] ("Plaintiff"), and _____ [Defendant's Name] ("Defendant").

Recitals

WHEREAS, Plaintiff filed a civil action against Defendant, [County Name] [Court Name] Court Case Number [Case number] (the "Civil Case"); and

WHEREAS, to avoid the time and expense of litigation, the Parties desire to resolve their differences and reach a compromise and settlement for all disputes existing and potentially existing between them relating to a debt owed by Defendant to Plaintiff.

Agreement

In consideration of the mutual execution of this Agreement and the releases and promises made in this Agreement by the Parties, the Parties hereby agree as follows:

1. In exchange for complete resolution of this matter, Defendant shall pay to Plaintiff $_____. This payment (the "Settlement Amount") will be paid in trust for the benefit of Plaintiff to _____ [Plaintiff's Law Firm] upon execution of this Agreement and completion of the terms outlined in paragraph 2.

2. _____ ("Plaintiff's Attorney") shall provide the original of this Agreement, executed by Plaintiff, to Defendant's attorney [or Defendant]. Defendant's attorney [or Defendant] will then have the Settlement Amount sent to Plaintiff's Attorney. Upon receipt of the Settlement Amount by Plaintiff's Attorney, and subject to those funds clearing the bank and becoming available for disbursal by Plaintiff's Attorney, Plaintiff shall submit to Defendant's attorney [or Defendant] a signed Request for Dismissal of the Civil Case with prejudice as to the entirety of the Civil Case, with each side to bear their own attorneys' fees and costs. Plaintiff further agrees that it will not attempt to refile the Civil Case, or any portion of it in the same or any other jurisdiction. Once the foregoing has occurred, Plaintiff's Attorney may disburse funds from the Settlement Funds to Plaintiff.

3. Plaintiff agrees to report the Account of Debtor's as "Paid in Full" to all credit bureaus, and shall refrain from reporting any negative credit information regarding Debtor's Account.

4. This Agreement constitutes a compromise, settlement, and release of disputed claims and is being entered into solely to

avoid the burden, inconvenience, and expense of litigating those claims.

5. The Parties agree to act in good faith and to cooperate fully with each other in carrying out the intent of this Agreement, and for that purpose agree to execute all additional documents as may prove reasonably necessary to accomplish that intent.

6. The Parties shall each bear their own costs and attorney fees incurred in connection with this Agreement, and each waives the right to make a claim against the other for such costs, attorney fees or any other expenses associated with the matters being settled herein.

7. The failure of any Party at any time to require performance of any provision of this Agreement shall not limit that Party's right to enforce the provision, nor shall any waiver of any breach of any provision constitute a waiver of that provision itself.

8. The Parties hereby incorporate the Recitals set forth above as an integral part of this Agreement and acknowledge the truth and accuracy of those Recitals.

9. This Agreement is the entire, final, and complete agreement of the Parties relating to the subject of this Agreement, and supersedes and replaces all prior or existing written and oral agreements between the Parties or their representatives relating thereto. No amendment or modification of this Agreement shall be effective unless in a written document executed by all Parties whose interests are affected by the modification. Any controversy arising under this Agreement shall be governed by and construed in accordance with the laws of the State of _____.

10. If any provision of this Agreement is held to be invalid or unenforceable, all remaining provisions will continue in full force and effect.

11. This Agreement may be executed in multiple counterparts, all of which shall be deemed originals, and with the same effect as if all Parties had signed the same document. All of such counterparts shall be construed together with and shall constitute one Agreement, but in making proof, it shall only be necessary to produce one such counterpart. A facsimile transmission shall be as valid and enforceable as an original.

12. This Agreement shall inure to the benefit of and be binding upon the heirs, legal representatives, successors and assigns of the Parties.

The Parties, by their signatures below, have executed this Agreement and agree to be bound by it.

Dated: _____

PLAINTIFF

_____

DEFENDANT

_____

RESTRICTIVE ENDORSEMENT FOR BACK OF PERSONAL CHECK WITHOUT HAVING A SETTLEMENT AGREEMENT

This check constitutes full payment of all claims by the Payee hereof against _____ [Debtor's Name] and the endorsement of this check is a full and complete release of all claims of the Payee against _____ [Debtor's Name]. Any alteration of this check or this endorsement shall render this check null and void.

NOTE: This endorsement is not recommended and may not be enforceable as explained in Chapter 8.

RESTRICTIVE ENDORSEMENT FOR BACK OF CASHIER'S CHECK OR MONEY ORDER WHEN SETTLEMENT PAYMENT IS TO BE MADE TO CREDITOR

Cashing the enclosed check [or money order] represents payment in full of account number _____ and constitutes your acceptance of the Release & Settlement Agreement dated _____ and all of its terms.

Made in the USA
Columbia, SC
05 August 2017